HAPPINESS
COMES IN
WAVES

LIFE LESSONS FROM THE OCEAN

Holly Daniels Christensen

ROCK
POINT

© 2022 by Quarto Publishing Group USA Inc.

Photography © Samantha Robshaw Photography Pages 46-47, 60-61, 64-65, 68-69, 70-71, 75, 106-107 ,114-115, 116-117, 122-123, 129, 139, 150-151, 152-153, 165, 178-179

All other photography © Shutterstock

First published in 2022 by Rock Point, an imprint of The Quarto Group, 142 West 36th Street, 4th Floor, New York, NY 10018, USA T (212) 779-4972 F (212) 779-6058 www.Quarto.com

Rock Point titles are also available at discount for retail, wholesale, promotional, and bulk purchase. For details, contact the Special Sales Manager by email at specialsales@quarto.com or by mail at The Quarto Group, Attn: Special Sales Manager, 100 Cummings Center Suite 265D, Beverly, MA 01915 USA.

10 9 8 7 6 5 4 3

ISBN: 978-1-63106-776-1

Library of Congress Control Number: 2021947620

Publisher: Rage Kindelsperger
Creative Director: Laura Drew
Senior Managing Editor: Cara Donaldson
Project Editor: Keyla Pizarro-Hernández
Cover and Interior Design: Tara Long

Printed in China

This book provides general information with various widely known and widely accepted images that tend to evoke feelings of strength and confidence. However, it should not be relied upon as recommending or promoting any specific diagnosis or method of treatment for a particular condition, and it is not intended as a substitute for medical advice or for direct diagnosis and treatment of a medical condition by a qualified physician. Readers who have questions about a particular condition, possible treatments for that condition, or possible reactions from the condition or its treatment should consult a physician or other qualified healthcare professional.

TO LEXA AND LYLA, you're everything good in this world.
Always remember, the universe will take care of you.

TO ERIC, thank you for endlessly believing in my potential. I love you.

TO DANIELLE, there are no words to express my gratitude.
Thank you for being an incredible thought partner throughout
this process. I couldn't have done it without you.

TO MY DAD, it's been a tall order watching over me from heaven
for the past thirty-seven years, but damn, you've done a great job.
Thank you for keeping me safe and allowing me to find happiness.
I miss you every day.

contents

INTRODUCTION

WHEN I WAS A YOUNG CHILD GROWING UP ON CAPE COD, I found the ocean to be fascinating, magical, and messy in the best way possible. The little crabs pinching at my toes, letting me know without a doubt that this was their turf; the tiny translucent minnows always swimming *just* out of reach every time I thought I had caught one in my net. I remember the surge of hopeful anticipation that I would feel each time I plunged my net into the salty ocean water, only to be met with dramatic childhood disappointment every time I realized over and over again that my net was empty. This activity could go on for hours, and when I finally did catch and release one of those minnows, the pure delight I felt was incredible.

I grew to love the beach not only for surfing, splashing, and swimming as a child but also for the peaceful, patient calm it lent me in times of turmoil as an adult. The smell, the sounds, and the surrounding vibrations always bring me back to being the playful, confident little girl I was before life got tough. Not only am I grateful for the healing power of the sea, but I'm also blessed that it has been a guide for me to discover my calling in life. I am forever connected to the water.

My journey has been extraordinarily colorful, from dropping out of high school and leaving home at the age of fifteen, to holding over fifty different jobs throughout my twenties (sometimes three at a time) to keep a roof over my head, to battling the most severe case of Graves' disease that my doctor had ever seen, somehow knowing that there was light at the end of the tunnel. Through it all, I always remembered what the ocean taught me as a child, and I used that to keep moving forward, one foot in front of the other, through every challenge. Now I'm the grateful owner and CEO of an eleven-year-old small business that motivates and excites me every single day.

I discovered sand as an artistic medium about fifteen years ago. My childhood best friend had a successful small business creating ornaments using sand from our favorite beaches on Cape Cod and I was working with her to expand that business. She suggested we take a jewelry-making class at a local studio and the rest is history—I fell in love! I learned multiple ways to inlay sand and other earth elements into precious metals and I began making jewelry for friends and family at my kitchen table.

As soon as word got around, people began bringing me a few grains of sand from their travels for personalized designs. I started to notice how extraordinarily unique each sampling of sand or earth was from different locations around the world. The colors and textures are vast and varied and the energy it holds is eternal. It's been part of the Earth since the dawn of time and is comprised of rock, quartz, shell, crystals, coral, and other weathered material. Not only that, but there are so many iconic and memorable destinations around the world that hold deep sentimental value for travelers and beach enthusiasts. The emotional reaction that people had to my creations in the beginning was something that moved me deeply.

I would hear stories of weddings, childhood beach homes, favorite vacation spots with loved ones every summer, ashes being sprinkled on the shore, honeymoon moments, first kisses, and so much more. This is what gave me the confidence and passion to follow my dreams and launch Dune Jewelry & Co. in 2010. I knew it was my calling to capture all of these stories and life experiences in tangible reminders that people could wear forever. Now, eleven years later, my business handcrafts jewelry and accessories from over five thousand destinations around the world. Customers can also send their own sand or elements from a special place or moment in time. Our mantra is "live for the moment, then take it with you."

Mother Earth is one of the greatest gifts we have and taking care of her should be on our "today list," every day. It is my belief that inside every woman lies the true, authentic, and wild soul of the ocean, and therefore from the ocean we can learn. She is the life force of our planet, differentiating us from all others. She is nurturing and complex and when we tap into her depths, it is there that we can find the knowledge to live authentically with true and honest connection to the Earth and ourselves.

The ocean never apologizes for her wild ways, and she is forever appreciated for the whole of her, not simply a "good or bad" moment she may have, but the entire volume of beauty, nourishment, and peace she brings to this Earth; so, shouldn't we regard ourselves confidently the same way? As a multifaceted and wondrous creature? The unequivocal answer is "yes!" As women, we are wondrous, we are complex, and we deserve to live truthful, authentic lives that honor our inner dialogue and bring us joy in the process. Come along on this journey with me and learn why I believe wholeheartedly that *happiness comes in waves.*

The lessons in this book are meant to help you expand your love of the water and create a life full of joy. Each of the lessons are things that I've learned as a beach lover, mom, business owner, and sand connoisseur that I hope you will find useful. Carry the lessons with you as you journey along many of life's transitions. As you go through each chapter, you will also find powerful quotes and sand stories from empowered women around the globe. I've also included short meditations at the end of each chapter to help you love yourself more and quiet your inner critic by staying positively connected with nature.

I hope this book brings you closer to the water in ways that you haven't thought of before and encourages you to embrace the ebb and flow of life.

With love and sandy hands,

Holly Daniels Christensen

BE
UNSTOPPABLE

Be like the waves of the ocean. Set your destination, and don't stop moving until you get there.

NICOLE MICHELLE, RECORDING ARTIST

sand story

After losing our jobs, my husband proposed moving our small family to Florida. We'd discussed, as many New Yorkers do, making the move for an easier pace and more affordable lifestyle, but that was just a dream, right? This was scarier than the job loss, but with some reservation, I agreed. On the day we arrived, before unpacking one box, we drove to the beach. As we passed the mangroves and emerged onto the sand, the wonder on my daughter's face put everything into perspective. She stood with her gaze fixed on the ocean as the waves wildly crashed onto the sand. I knew then that we had won. We were given what others just dream about. We were forced to take a chance and make a change. The beach always had my heart, but on that day the ebb and flow of the tide forever became a reminder of life's patterns. Whether gently lapping or furiously clapping, jump in and ride the waves.

—Nicole Borriello,

Fitness Professional, Intuitive Healer, and Risk Taker

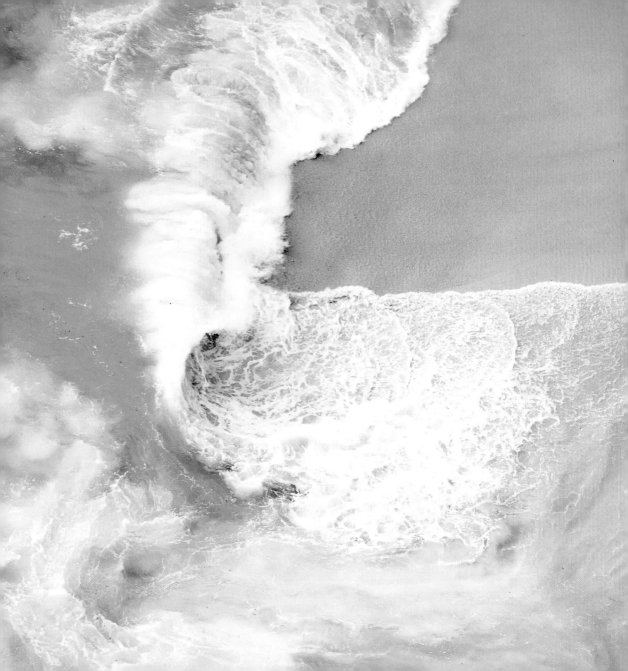

Just as the ocean is the life force of our planet, women are the life force of humanity.

SAMANTHA ROBSHAW, PHOTOGRAPHER, WANDERER

a lesson in waves

Every day without fail, the Earth, the moon, and the ocean dance in harmony with rhythmic precision. These are, as we all know them, the high and low tides that occur like clockwork across our globe each day. Similarly, I believe that we have our own inner tides that flow within our bodies on a daily basis. Just think of the energy that courses through your body as you start your day. Sometimes you're flying high, feeling focused, clear, and motivated, while other times, you are vibrating low, feeling fuzzy, foggy, uncertain, and uninspired. I like to refer to these feelings as our high tides and low tides. When we learn to harness the momentum of our high tides while honoring the drift of our low tides, we can step into our power and find the balance to succeed.

When we take the time to connect more deeply with ourselves, we start to understand who we are and what we want out of our lives, what brings us joy, and what drains our energy. We can discover our purpose and what drives us, what allows our tides to surge and move forward and what holds us back. And when we know what our purpose is, we can decide to go after our wildest dreams—to live a life full of motivated passion and become a force of nature.

I've always believed that our lives have many similarities to the ocean. There are calm days that bring joy and inspiration and there are stormy days that bring tears, pain, and sorrow. Water is unstoppable in all of its forms and unpredictable—like much of life. But it always finds a way to flow and push through with gentle force. Just like the ocean, there are storms we will never be ready for and hardships that will not be easy to navigate, but it's important to recognize that these moments in time rarely last forever. Often, it's during the most difficult times in our lives that we learn the greatest lessons, which propel us into our most magical moments. Pushing through and weathering the storm is where we learn how incredibly powerful we really are.

{ LEARNING MORE ABOUT OUR INTERNAL FLOW IS KEY TO INCREASING PRODUCTIVITY AND HAPPINESS WHILE EMBRACING OUR LIMITLESS POTENTIAL.

Think of the days when you feel in control of your life. You're joyful, energized, and powerful. You look good, you feel good, you exude confidence in every important moment. That's your high tide. Take note of it. Grab your journal and write down which day of the week it is, the date, how much sleep you had the night before, what time you woke up, what your diet has been like, and other notable things that have happened to you during the day.

The ocean does not apologize for its depth and the mountains do not seek forgiveness for the space they take and so, neither shall I.

BECCA LEE, POET

I like to capture every ounce of information, which can take some time, but it's worth it. The more details you document, the more you can learn what is sparking positivity and confidence in your everyday life.

> ALLOW YOURSELF GRACE AND KNOW THAT THERE'S ALWAYS A WAVE OF GOODNESS RIGHT AROUND THE CORNER.

On the other side of your water energy are the low-tide days. That's when you're not as energetic or maybe you have some feelings of self-doubt or fear. You have to know that this is okay! Your low tides are perfectly normal, and we all have them. There will always be days or moments that are difficult to get through or situations that will be uncomfortable and drain your energy. During low tides, document it the same way you've collected your high-tide information. Use these times to learn and give yourself the self-care that you need. Find ways to ground yourself and relax, and remember when days like this arrive, anything goes! Binge-watch your favorite TV shows, snuggle up and read a book, order your favorite meal—twice if you want to. It's your body telling you that you need to pause, take a moment to reflect, and indulge a bit.

I firmly believe that when you show yourself kindness, especially through periods of adversity, you are using your time wisely to heal and reinforce unconditional love for yourself. Make sure you listen to your needs—they are valid. Taking a pause will refresh your energy so that you can keep going and come back stronger tomorrow. By understanding and nurturing what your body needs, you are giving yourself the courage to become an incredible force.

Much of our life is spent trying to bring order out of seeming chaos. We want predictability and regularity in a world where randomness and chance seem to rule. You can't always control what will happen next, but you can control how you respond to the situation. If you take time to understand what your inner self needs, you are learning how to push through during times of adversity, whether it is a difficult breakup, a challenging day at work, a fight with a loved one, or a tragedy that came out of nowhere. This helps us respond to those days with a healthy perspective. The better we know ourselves and our needs, the better we can navigate life.

Let your inner tides guide you to discover the power within, so like the ocean you too can become unstoppable.

The ocean was vast like her determination, and while the waves crashed upon her, she continued to rise above the surface.

AMBER JEWEL WAX, FASHION BLOGGER

AN UNSTOPPABLE
wave meditation

Find a comfortable place to stand or sit and close your eyes. Imagine yourself at the beach or near a body of water on a warm summer day. Your personal body of water can be a lake, a pond, a stream, or a waterfall. Begin to feel the soft breeze on your face and the warm earth beneath you. Notice the fresh air and the sound of birds overhead while listening to the water flow around you. Take a deep breath in through your nose, filling your lungs to the top of your breath. Breathe out through your mouth, emptying your lungs. Repeat this exercise two more times and say silently or aloud to yourself, "I am capable of great things; I am unstoppable." Repeat this mantra two more times while harnessing the energy of the water that surrounds you, flowing endlessly and with purpose. Take one more breath in and exhale through your mouth. Slowly begin to open your eyes and allow your mind and body to settle. Thank the water for its gentle force and endless wisdom.

BE
ABUNDANT

THE OCEAN CAN BE A SOURCE OF PROFOUND BEAUTY, CALM, AND PEACE. HOWEVER, ON MOTHER NATURE'S WHIM IT MAY TURN INTO A VIOLENT BEAST, CAPABLE OF UNCONTAINED DESTRUCTION. AS HUMAN BEINGS, WE HAVE THE PRIVILEGE OF DISCERNMENT, WHICH GRANTS US THE ABILITY AND RESPONSIBILITY TO DRAW UPON OUR ABUNDANT POWERS AND RESOURCES WITH PURPOSE AND RESTRAINT.

NICOLE AMATO, FOUNDER, AMATOSTYLE

sand story

In the daily grind of life, it's sometimes easy to forget that we must stop and take stock of where we have been, where we are now, and where we are going. Having grown up in England, that meant many wonderful, yet often chilly family holidays with my parents and brother in St. Ives, Cornwall. I fondly remember our Cornish ice cream being stolen by cheeky seagulls as we ran across the beach to the trampolines! And now, more recently, it means special times making memories here in the United States with my lovely little family and friends: days out swimming, playing baseball, and grilling at Plymouth Long Beach; watching the determination of my son as he surfs, while my husband and I sit with our toes in the sand, breathing in life and sea air! Looking out into the ocean during these moments, I feel grateful for all we've built together. And, as my oceanside memories transport me back to these various phases of my life, of time spent with loved ones, my heart feels full, and my life rich with experiences and love.

-Kate Colozzi

Director of Sales and Events, Mum, Wanderer

The river is not lost when it joins the sea; vaster, wilder, it flows on. Why would it be different for us?

KATIE SIMPSON, TEACHER, YOGA INSTRUCTOR

a lesson in waves

Have you ever stood right at the ocean's edge at low tide with your toes kissing the small, playful waves? There have been many times I've stood just like that, looking out at the horizon with intense wonder and a full, curious heart. The ocean feeds us, heals us, gives us joy, and quite literally connects us to other countries around the world. Somehow, the water also has a special way of connecting us back to ourselves and making us feel like the present moment is all we will ever need. Allowing yourself to live in the moment and come from a place of "I have everything I need" instead of "I need more" opens your heart and allows abundance to come to you freely and effortlessly.

When we first think of the word *abundance* and what it means, many people simply think of money and material possessions, but this is just a small piece of it—a tiny harbor in the infinite ocean. An abundance of money and material possessions can obviously be a good thing because it provides stability as well as greater opportunities to explore the world and further your education. It's hard to focus on manifesting any type of abundance if we're constantly worried about paying the rent or where our next meal is coming from. Let's agree that creating financial abundance is important, not because money alone will bring you happiness, but because money can provide a sense of security and open doors to other forms of abundance. It's important to remember that there are so many ways to live a rich, healthy, happy life that don't revolve around gaining material items or spending money. Quite often, a well-planned experience is going to be far more fulfilling than a new outfit or toy to play with.

ABUNDANCE CAN TAKE SHAPE AND MANIFEST ITSELF IN YOUR LIFE IN DIFFERENT WAYS.

But what does abundance really mean? It means that you are fulfilled in every avenue in your life. It means your soul, spirit, mind, and heart are content. When you allow yourself to recognize the abundance of your potential, you're giving yourself permission to live a life full of purpose. When I first started my business, we didn't make a significant amount of money for the first four years, but I still felt satisfied and happy because I was doing work that I absolutely loved and took pride in. When you recognize the parts of your life that you love and begin to shift your focus to appreciate them, you are inviting abundance to enter your life while also fostering inner growth. By appreciating all of the simple pleasures that surround you, you are reducing negativity and banishing extra stress and anxiety from your daily routine.

Similar to how the sea emits peaceful energy before a storm, I find my lulls at work to be immediately followed by a downpour of opportunities. A little silence means something huge is around the corner.

CAROLINE KARWOSKI, MODEL, NFL CHEERLEADER

I truly believe that a positive mind-set can transform the entire trajectory of your life. When I first started Dune Jewelry, it never once occurred to me that I might not succeed. I was young and endlessly optimistic. Even when something bad happened I would find a way to turn it around and create a more positive result. It was from that type of energy (and a whole lot of hard work) that my business became successful. When you automatically think a situation is going to have a bad result, it's easy to spiral downward. But when you envision events in your life playing out positively, you truly begin to manifest your desired outcome. It's so important to practice gratitude and celebrate every single win, big or small. I love to write down at least one thing that I'm grateful for every morning.

{ APPRECIATE THE LITTLE THINGS AND THANK THE UNIVERSE FOR EVERYTHING IT PROVIDES TO YOU.

It's a quick and easy habit that you can do too. Write down at least one thing you're grateful for each day, and you'll begin seeing the world from a different perspective.

Courage is another useful tool that allows abundance to enter your life. People who live in a place of fear often have low expectations and will settle for less than they desire because they don't believe that they *deserve* a favorable outcome. As a business owner, I have always believed in coming from a place of "yes", then figuring it out later. In doing so, it has opened many doors along the way. Being courageous isn't necessarily about doing big, outlandish things—it's about doing little things that interest you that are just outside of your comfort zone. If it scares you but you go for it anyway and then succeed, it feels incredible!

While sometimes you may fail at something new, you will always learn from a failure, which in turn becomes a win. Bravery is about doing the things you're most passionate about even if you are unsure of the outcome. It may not always work out how you planned, but it will always be a worthy experience. There will be moments when hardships and worries will inevitably creep in, but by practicing abundance, you won't allow negative thoughts or feelings to control you and become part of you. The more you have the courage to accept opportunities that are presented to you, the more abundance you will attract into your life.

So, go ahead, dip your toe in and see how it feels. You won't regret it.

May gratitude erupt within your soul followed by a tsunami of knowledge that YOU are more than enough.

JOLI BOUCHER, INSTRUCTIONAL TECHNOLOGY SPECIALIST, GARDENER, DREAMER

A WAVE OF
abundance meditation

Find a comfortable place to sit or stand, preferably with close access to nature. Close your eyes and imagine yourself on a sandy beach with an empty pail and shovel. Grab your imaginary shovel and scoop up the beach sand as you breathe in while thinking about something you're grateful for. As you exhale, imagine pouring your scoop of sand into the empty pail. The sand flows gently and easily. Repeat this until you have a pail full of gratitude. Feel yourself come to center and relax into your body. Continue to take a few more deep breaths in and out and finish with the mantra "I am abundant; I have everything I need." Say this silently to yourself or aloud if you prefer. Take one last deep breath and slowly open your eyes. Give thanks to the universe for the abundance it provides and carry that gratitude through the rest of your day.

BE LIGHT

sand story

The beach has always been such an important part of me and my soul since I was a very little girl. I have precious memories spent at the beach with my grandmother, daughter, and husband building sandcastles, collecting seashells and sea glass . . . sitting and walking on the beach always clears my mind and carries my worries away, leaving a feeling of lightness and peace. At every beach, my toes have savored the sand. That sand has become mysteriously sacred. I have the seashells and sand from our honeymoon in Bermuda, from the first time our daughter went to the beach in Florida, from a trip we won to Aruba, and from a romantic sunset vow renewal at the beach on Sanibel Island for our thirtieth wedding anniversary. The beach will always be my happy place.

—Linda Burke

Wave Maker, Dune Jewelry Enthusiast

> "

The darkest of nights, the roughest ocean storms, the thickest of forests– they all eventually lead to light.

VANESSA COPPES, MOM, CEO, AUTHOR, ENTREPRENEUR, AND WILD WOMAN

> "

a lesson in waves

There is no light without darkness, and when you carry your own inner light and reflect it outward generously to the world around you, it helps to raise the vibration of authentic positivity. The world becomes brighter, healthier, and full of hopeful possibilities—not only for you, but for those around you too.

Isn't it amazing how the ocean and our mind, with their different regions of light and dark, share so many similarities? The light part of the ocean near the surface is much like the conscious part of our brain. The surface is where all of the action happens. It's the home of spectacular sea life, it's where we can see our reflection in a small tidepool at low tide. It's where we swim, play, and blissfully watch dolphins break out of the water with a rainbow arc. Joy radiates and surfers relish every swell. It's light, bright, and breezy, and for many of us, this is where we prefer to stay, always in the light.

But it's important to note that the ocean wouldn't survive without its darker depths. Below the surface is a fundamental ecosystem integral to feeding the lighter part of the sea. The depths of the ocean are kindred to our unconscious mind—hidden from view but incredibly powerful. The majority of what we do, think, and feel is dictated by our subconscious. It is said to be the source of our feelings and emotional reactions. Besides joy and happiness, it can also contain emotional baggage and long-lost scars that stem from childhood trauma or even from current events that you're presently dealing with.

> IT'S IMPORTANT TO OUR MENTAL HEALTH TO RECOGNIZE THE LIGHT AND DARK PARTS OF OUR PSYCHE AND WORK DILIGENTLY TO CREATE BALANCE.

Thousands of thoughts cross our mind every day, and they are of varying degrees of light and dark, good and bad. Most negative thoughts are largely hidden from the conscious mind. If negative thoughts are not confronted, they can sow some serious damage, but when approached with the right mind-set, they can be the very thing that leads to your brightest moments. Therapy, meditation, and personal and professional coaching are wonderful ways of resolving internal issues. We're human, and all of us can be emotionally triggered by words, phrases, images, or memories. The point is to know why and how you react to such triggers. Bringing it all to the surface will help you gain power over your life and resolve any lingering darkness.

The sun reflecting off the surface of the ocean is the light we should reflect back into the world and to one another.

RAINA PATRICIA, OCEAN LOVER,
SUNSET CHASER, MOTHER, AND NFL WIFE

For many years, I was ashamed that I dropped out of high school and left home at fifteen years old. Healing is a lifelong journey, and this brought me so much darkness that I never spoke a word about it until a few years ago. My father had passed when I was eight years old, and my mother subsequently suffered from an extreme addiction that she could never get a hold of. My home life became unhealthy and unmanageable. So, in an effort to move toward the lighter part of the ocean, I left and never looked back. This worked for a while, but eventually I realized that that part of my life will always be a part of me and I couldn't keep it submerged forever. I began journaling and talking about it with friends and family and it dawned on me that my past doesn't predict my future. The more I talked about it and normalized it within my own mind, the more it became a simple part of me—a moment in time that helped mold me, but doesn't define me. All of those challenging, dark memories have led me to an extraordinary life that I'm forever grateful to live. Each moment helped me evolve and taught me about the type of wife, mother, and human being that I want to be.

So, what are the best ways to bring the light? While it's important to put in the work and use therapy and coaching to develop and grow, there are also some instant ways to put your mind in a better place. Spend time out in nature; I love the saying, "Salt water heals all." Take the time to travel to a beach and look out at the ocean. Let the sound of the waves wash over you. While there,

build sandcastles, take a long walk on the sand, read a book or magazine that you love, search for beach treasures, journal it out, or simply stare at the infinite sky, watching the clouds pass by. If getting to the beach is completely impossible, try to do similar things at a park or a lake.

If you're stuck at home, you can play a game, color in a coloring book, or belt out your favorite song in the shower. Spend time doing something you love that makes you laugh or brings you joy. Another trick is to do something nice for someone else. Or how about complimenting a stranger out of the blue? You can make someone's day by simply being kind. It feels amazing to give something so small and see the happiness (or surprise) that washes over the recipient.

Be the light in someone else's day and feel the waves of life become gentler, softer, happier.

The sea is the most dependable friend you will ever have. It will never spill your secrets, it will never judge you, and it will always be there to light your way.

GEORGIA SHURTLEFF, AUNTIE, FRIEND, DANCER, AND JELLYFISH

A WAVE OF
light meditation

Find a comfortable position and get still. Close your eyes as you begin to deepen your breath and imagine yourself standing in the ocean. The warm sun is on your face and the water surrounding you is the perfect temperature. Let your mind run free for a moment as you continue to take deep breaths in and out. Accept and acknowledge any thought that comes into focus and then allow the calm, soothing waves to wash them away. There is no need to identify with the thoughts that come up. Just simply let them have their moment and let them go. If you get stuck on a particular thought, use the mantra "I am not my thoughts; I am light" to bring yourself back to center. Bring yourself back to the water around you and imagine submerging yourself fully in the healing, salty ocean. As you return to the surface, take one last deep breath in and out. Slowly open your eyes and thank Mother Earth for the light she provides.

All life comes from the deep, nourishing waters of the sea. When you embrace the ebb and flow of change with wisdom, courage, and grace, inspiration will flow. Smile as you seek the divine within yourself and create and transform in the process.

MARILYN BALL, RADIO/PODCAST HOST, TRAVELER, DAUGHTER OF THE SEA

sand story

Growing up on Cape Cod, I was lucky to have a beach within walking distance from my home. It was there that I was happiest as a kid . . . mucking around in the mudflats and jumping off into the ocean to get clean, only to get muddy again while climbing back up. On the days I didn't feel like getting dirty, I would patiently walk along the shoreline and explore the delicate tidal pools for hermit crabs (or "hermies," as I would call them), periwinkles, and other little sea creatures, taking them into my hands and studying them closely. Getting right down into the ocean allows you to experience a whole other world, one that has many lessons to take with you. Sometimes you have to dive in with both feet. Get a little dirty. Look closer to find the things that will inspire you.

—Moira Garcia
Dune Jewelry Sales Guru

> **"** Sometimes coming up with a new idea or the starting point of a new project, I feel like I'm banging my head against the wall. Really, all I need is to stick my head in the water and listen to the waves and let inspiration wash over me.
>
> LAUREN BEHNING, BRAND MANAGER, DUNE JEWELRY **"**

a lesson in waves

With the ocean's eternal beauty on display and a million of its species in a constant state of cooperation and competition, there is bound to be something that moves your soul. You could easily catch a glimpse of a great wave the likes of which you've never seen. You might spot a new fish or curious sea creature. There's bound to be a sunset that takes your breath away when the sun kisses the horizon, or a sunrise you'll never forget. Whatever you encounter, the endless enchantment of the ocean makes it hard not to feel inspired. The power of the ocean has a way of reminding us that we are the creators of our own lives, that we are braver than we believe, and that we can accomplish anything we put our mind to.

What inspires you and how can you develop that feeling into a thriving passion? If you are a bit unsure of where your true interests lie and how to make them come alive, try out different things to see what creates a spark. Be open to unique possibilities. Say "yes" to something new and step into an unknown path with bravery. You don't have to be on a grand adventure for life to be inspiring; in fact, isn't life alone the grandest adventure of all? A spark of inspiration can come from something as small as starting research on a new career path or writing the first sentence to the book you've been conjuring up. Or you can find it in something *huge*, like moving to a new city or saying "I love you" for the very first time. Grab a journal and write down what makes you smile and what genuinely fascinates you, then forge forward with small action steps to make those things happen. If you're having a hard time getting started with a journal, you can purchase one that includes prompts to help get your creativity flowing.

{ INSPIRATION IS EVERYWHERE; YOU SIMPLY NEED TO ALLOW YOURSELF TO SEE IT.

Take action to make your dreams a reality. Put together a plan. If you don't know where to start, broaden your horizons by taking a road trip, getting back to nature, visiting a library, listening to a new podcast, or taking an art class. By opening yourself up to the many possibilities the world has to offer, you will receive the kind of guidance you seek.

THERE IS NOTHING LIKE YOUR TOES IN THE SAND AND WAVES WASHING OVER YOUR BODY TO MAKE YOU FEEL A PART OF THIS BIG WIDE WORLD. THE WATER HAS THIS AMAZING POWER. I ALWAYS LEAVE FEELING REJUVENATED AND INSPIRED KNOWING THAT I CAN DO ANYTHING!

DEANNE CAPOTOSTO, PROFESSIONAL ORGANIZER, TRAVELER AND SWIMMER

One way I love to stay motivated is by creating a vision board. Take a large poster board and cover it with photos, literature, brands, names, and mantras that focus on the kind of person you want to be, the kind of things you want to do, and the kind of things you want to have. I know someone who fills her board with gorgeous pictures of where she wants to visit, the car of her dreams, and the qualities of the person she wants to attract someday. There is a saying that the mind attracts what it focuses on, and a vision board could be just the thing to get you there. Start envisioning your desired future. Put your board in a prominent place where you can see it. Whenever you feel doubts creeping in, look at the board to remind you of the bigger picture.

To help you get started in creating a vision board, ask yourself these questions:

- What do I value most?

- What do I want out of life?

- Where do I see myself in five years?

- When do I feel most joyful?

- What is my most fabulous dream?

- If I knew I wouldn't fail, what would I do tomorrow?

You could be realizing your dreams sooner than you think. I always tell my daughter Lyla to envision how it will feel when she nails one of her gymnastics moves at her meets. She gives me a little eye roll at first, but she takes my advice and always thanks me for it afterward. When you allow yourself to open up to everything that's available to you, you become the best version of yourself. And when you're able to be your best self by embracing who you are and manifesting your dreams, you are able to inspire others as well. All ships rise with the tide, and the more we can inspire the world around us, the more positivity we can bring to fruition.

{ DON'T LET FEAR OR DOUBTS STOP YOU FROM MOVING FORWARD IN CREATING THE LIFE YOU WANT FOR YOURSELF.

There's nothing like lighting up the lives of those around you by sharing your life story and unique ideas. You can make a mark on the world by simply being you. Do it from a place of integrity and passion and try not to care too much about what others might think. I promise that you can help those around you by being authentically who you are.

Like a lighthouse guiding a ship to shore, your creativity and ideas can be a beacon for others.

"

With all the highs and lows that life brings I see myself reflected in the resilient ocean waves. I find it endlessly inspiring that as many times as they fall, they always rise again.

DANIELLE GODJIKIAN, EXECUTIVE ASSISTANT, NATURE LOVER

"

A WAVE OF
inspiration meditation

Close your eyes and take a deep breath in. Pause for a second at the top of your breath and then exhale any pent-up energy in your body. Repeat until a sense of calm washes over you. Begin to envision the life of your dreams. Picture your dream home by the ocean, in the mountains, or wherever it is that inspires you most. Picture the art and decor you have on the walls. Imagine walking barefoot along the hardwood, carpet, or tile. Visualize yourself walking to the door and as you step outside, you are surrounded by what stirs your soul, whether it's an abundance of peaceful nature or a city filled with excitement and energy. Breathe in and repeat the mantra "I am living the life of my dreams; I am deeply inspired by all that is around me," and then breathe out. Take a few more moments in your dream home, then take one last deep breath, open your eyes slowly, and thank the universe for all of the brilliance it provides.

BE
AUTHENTIC

Empowerment starts with embracing your inner waves. You are the captain.

TIFFANY RICE, SPIRIT MEDIUM

sand story

There are moments when I catch myself daydreaming about my summers at the Jersey Shore, where the sand and the ocean hold a special place in my heart. Some of my favorite moments were spent with my dad, when we would stand in the water talking for hours. The beach is where I met and fell in love with my husband and where we got engaged. I remember driving with a friend once and she said, "Let's drive until the map turns blue." That stuck with me and makes me smile just thinking about it! One thing I know for sure is I will always be that little girl from the Jersey Shore, carrying a bucket full of shells with saltwater in my hair and a golden tan. Do yourself a favor, if you get the opportunity: grab a friend and drive until the map turns blue . . . you will be glad you did!

—*Carole Imperiale*

Publicist, 2x Cancer Survivor, and Beach Lover

> **"**
>
> Explore the depths of your being and dive headfirst into the things that make you feel most alive. The world is an ocean of possibilities, as long as you never lose appreciation for the ground from which you came.
>
> **"**

JENNIFER DECILLIS, PUBLISHER, *BELLA MAGAZINE*

a lesson in waves

With the deliberate swoosh of its powerful waves, the water seems to tell us, "I'm here, and I'm going to be myself no matter what anyone thinks." The water moves how and where it wants. It breathes life into some of the world's most amazing creatures and sustains us all. The ocean understands its worth and therefore knows no reason to hold back. Like the ripples created by a drop of water falling into the ocean, your actions have a ripple effect on those around you, and even the smallest drop can create an impact. When you allow yourself to live your truth, you give others the permission to do the same. You can be like the ocean and create powerful ripples in your life, affecting people around you and even people you may never meet directly. It all begins with recognizing where you are holding back and allowing your true self to shine.

One of the biggest challenges in our adult lives is to live authentically without fear. After all, we are humans, and fear is part of our nature. We were conditioned from primitive times to watch out for wild animals, because otherwise we could be seriously hurt. But nowadays, in the age of social media, our fears have been taken to a completely different place and they have more to do with what other people think of us. We often put more stock in the risk of disapproval from others than the upside of listening to our own intuition, and that's why so often we shy away from acting authentically and true to our inner dialogue. We act and portray who we want our peers to believe we are, rather than risk the judgment we might endure if we reveal our genuine self.

> WE BECOME OUR OWN WORST ENEMY WHEN WE LET ANXIETY GUIDE OUR LIVES.

The riskiest things in life are often the ones we consider the scariest. Why? Because we think about the potential for failure and judgment, then we let fear take over. We are scared that we will fail at the things we want most, and it paralyzes us into believing that we aren't good enough. This fear can cloud our point of view and cause us to self-sabotage and miss great opportunities. It's essential to realize that we are all capable of great things—every single one of us—and our greatness has nothing to do with what other people think. It's based on our personal values, personality, ambition, and what's most important to us. Self-doubt and negative self-talk can keep us stuck in a lonely place. Living your life fearlessly is daunting, but millions of people do it every day—and you can too.

If you take risks, you allow your comfort zone to be so large it has its own beach house.

SUZANNE DWYER,
THE PRODUCTIVE BUSINESS DEVELOPMENT COACH

If you want to get to know yourself and don't know where to start, begin by looking at your belief systems. What do you value most? You can start by writing out simple words that mean a lot to you, like family, honesty, success, adventure, or love. Then create a plan to put those things in the forefront of your life. While doing this exercise, you may notice that the way you grew up has a lot to do with what you value or how you are living. Sometimes we act in accordance with a family dynamic, and we don't even realize it. If this dynamic is making you unhappy, then you may need to challenge your childhood and how you were raised.

{ **WHAT'S HOLDING YOU BACK?** Identify inconsistencies between your beliefs and your actions. You may want to accomplish something but find it difficult to do so. If you have difficulty following through, you need to find out why. Be sure to get introspective and listen to what your true self has to say, then start aligning your actions with your beliefs.

You can also identify the things you enjoy doing. Do you know what makes you happy? If not, then you may want to take more chances and explore different experiences. Say "yes" when opportunities present themselves, and perhaps say "no" to the things that are draining your energy and making you unhappy. Write down a list of all the things you do in a day, week, month. Circle everything that made you genuinely happy. During the next day, week, month, try to repeat those actions more frequently, and cut out the ones that bring you down or make you feel less like "you."

Living authentically isn't something that comes easily to many of us. We are trained to keep up with others, to live up to their expectations, and to judge ourselves according to societal standards. And while we may be inspired by other people, we should never compare ourselves to them. I promise that comparison will *never* make you feel better about yourself.

It may never seem like the right time to move toward your authentic self. There's a good chance you will continue to wonder whether you are adequate or special enough, or whether the time is right. Just remember one thing—life seldom presents you with all the "right" circumstances. What's most important is that *you* believe in yourself and your purpose. That's what will serve you in the long run.

It takes courage to brave new waters. Be like the ocean—bold, free, and true to her nature.

There is only one of you in this world. The horizon is limitless, and so is your potential. Be true to who you are. Powerful, unwavering, deep, and unapologetic– exactly like the ocean.

COURTENAY COOPER HALL,
FOUNDER OF *BELLA* MAGAZINE, BELLA TV AND MOM OF THREE

A WAVE OF
authenticity meditation

Use this meditation to tap into your truest self. Find a small tidepool at the beach with still water. You could even use a glass of water with sand at the bottom if you don't have access to the beach. The clear, still water represents your true self. Now imagine taking your finger and agitating the sand at the bottom and watch as it swirls around in the previously clear water. The sand floating in the water represents all of the thoughts, beliefs, and opinions you have learned through society. As the sand continues to swirl and begins to settle, take deep breaths in through your nose and out through your mouth. Repeat the mantra "I fearlessly and relentlessly embrace my true authentic self" as you watch the sand settle. Continue focusing on your breath and your mantra until the sand has fully settled. Take one last deep breath and express gratitude for the stillness and trust of the calm waters.

BE
ADVENTUROUS

It's true that the salt air can cure just about anything. But getting right down into the ocean allows you to experience a whole other world.

MOIRA GARCIA, DUNE JEWELRY SALES GURU

sand story

I parked in the lot at Reynisfjara Beach in Vik, Iceland, and walked out toward the ocean. It was my first stop after taking a red-eye from Boston and it was a heart-stopping, life-altering moment. The deep blue of the ocean and the spiky stacks of lava jutting out of the sea . . . it was like nothing I had ever seen. The crescent moon was visible in the low Arctic sun and the black sand was sparkling like diamonds under my boots. My eyes couldn't get enough. It was one of those moments in life where you stop, breathe it in, and do your best to remember it forever. Each grain of sand and every crashing wave is forever imprinted in my memory and heart. My hunger for adventure and travel has grown tenfold since then. There are a billion destinations before us, and I want to wear out the soles of my shoes trying to see each one.

—Samantha Robshaw

Adventurer, Photographer

To live blissfully in life, trust the flow and ride the waves; the great big ones always come.

DAWN DEL RUSSO, FASHION AND LIFESTYLE EXPERT,
FOUNDER OF BELLA DAWN BOUTIQUE
AND LIVETHEGLAMOUR.COM

,,

a lesson in waves

Have you ever heard of the polar bear plunge? Well, it's an adventure embarked upon by a group of spontaneous people of all ages, shapes, and sizes who jump into an ice-cold body of water on January 1st every year. The first recorded polar bear plunge was in Boston in 1904, and they've been doing it religiously ever since. Crazy? Maybe. Fun as heck? Yes! Many participants say that jumping into that freezing-cold water is the best way to start their year. It invigorates them like nothing they've ever experienced, and once they dry off and warm up, they feel fully "alive."

Embracing adventure, whether big or small, leads to a fulfilling life of fun and excitement. This means being open to all kinds of new possibilities and trying new things while doing your best to accept the unknown. It means questioning your current way of living and changing for the better. It means growing, expanding, evolving, and, in the process, maybe leaving something behind that no longer serves you. Caterpillars turn into butterflies. Snakes shed their skin more than four times per year. Children grow up and leave home to explore the world. These are just a few examples of natural, transformative experiences that are happening all around us.

It's important to note that I don't think we need to be reckless or take wildly dangerous risks to find adventure. Adventure can be found anywhere. An afternoon walk on a beautiful day can turn into bumping into an old friend you've been meaning to call. You could take your dog to the dog park and try out a new toy or ball and revel in your pet's joy. Maybe you find a ladybug on the windowsill in your office and instead of ignoring it, you take the time to count its spots and release it back outside. It's not always about going skydiving or cliff jumping.

IF YOU KEEP YOUR SENSE OF CURIOSITY, THE JOURNEY BECOMES A WHOLE LOT MORE INTERESTING, AND ADVENTURE WILL FIND YOU EVEN WHEN YOU LEAST EXPECT IT.

Most often we think of adventure as taking place in the external world. The first things that come to mind tend to be physical endeavors such as skydiving, road tripping, whitewater rafting, and other experiences that will get our adrenaline flowing, but adventure can also take place inside ourselves. We can go on an internal adventure that will last a lifetime as we get to know ourselves and find out who we really are. Some of us have the innate pull to explore the depths of our being, regardless of how we label our journey—spiritual, religious, philosophical, or psychological.

The ocean is a Mother–
a vessel of strength,
growth, and nurturing.
No matter where I wander
in the adventure of my life,
when I see her,
I know I am home.

JEN MUELLER, THERAPIST, DAYDREAMER, NATURE NERD

Did you know that 80 percent of the ocean is unexplored? There is always something new to be discovered, and like the ocean, there is a vastness within ourselves that is waiting to be explored. The most important thing you can do is be willing and open to learning about yourself and discovering your own depths. There is always something new to uncover, which makes our journey even more exciting. Like the ocean, there is adventure to be found right here inside ourselves as soon as we're ready to take the plunge.

Explore who you are at your core and discover your desires, your dislikes, and your purpose. Take yourself on a date—dinner and a movie solo. Get comfortable with yourself. Often, we find ourselves losing who we are as we prioritize other people and things in our lives. But you always need to make yourself a priority. Make time for yourself and for the things you enjoy doing. I know at times it can feel daunting to add one more thing to your calendar, but by adding things that you enjoy to your schedule and removing things that you don't, you are allowing adventure to enter into your life. Your "to-do" list should include things that bring value to you and your well-being. This will allow fresh and exciting opportunities to arise throughout your day. When you take care of your own needs, you are putting your best self out there into the world and giving the people you care about the best version of you.

SO MANY OF US FIND HEALTHY ADVENTURE IN THE WATER BECAUSE OF HOW EXHILARATING THE OCEAN CAN MAKE US FEEL.

If you have a dream but you aren't sure where to start or how to tap into this secret part of you, make a list of things you like to do or things you've always wanted to do and haven't tried yet. Want to go on an exotic vacation? Or get that career or business started? How about climbing Mount Kilimanjaro? Take small steps toward your goal by researching and planning. Put one foot in front of the other and once you have built a little momentum, you'll be ready to take the plunge and find your adventure. Jump in! A world full of opportunity awaits.

"

May you be driven toward adventure with the same strength and determination of a mighty wave toward the shore.

CHELDIN BARLATT RUMER, MOM AND
CEO/EXECUTIVE PRODUCER OF THIS IS IT NETWORK

"

A WAVE IN
adventure meditation

Sometimes it's difficult to step away from our daily routine, so here's a meditation to motivate you to embrace your own adventure. Slowly close your eyes and envision yourself on the sand listening to the waves and every sound around you. As you inhale the salt air, visualize a trip you may go on. It could be the brilliant views of Santorini, Greece, or maybe it's the turquoise waters of the Grand Cayman Islands. Exhale. This is your time to get connected to what suits your soul. Allow yourself to feel the warmth of the sun under your feet as you wander along the shore looking at the breathtaking views of the ocean. This is your time. This is your safe place. Adventure awaits as you move one foot in front of the other, allowing your heart to be free and your mind at ease. Take a deep inhale and exhale. Repeat three times. Whenever you need a mini-vacation, your adventure awaits. It's a mind-set away.

BE
CREATIVE

From growing up living on a boat to working now as a marine biologist, the ocean forever energizes me to stay curious and protect her endless wonders.

CANDACE CROSS, ASPIRING MARINE BIOLOGIST, DOCTORAL STUDENT

sand story

I have always grown up on or near a beach. Most of my summer memories as a child are of being on the beach playing in the sand, searching for seashells and sea glass, and swimming in the ocean. I remember dreaming of far-off adventures at sea and meeting mermaids along the way. The possibilities were endless. As I got older, I never wanted to lose those blissful feelings I had as a child, so I started traveling worldwide visiting the most unique beaches. I fell in love with the Caribbean. There is just something about the turquoise water and the soft silkiness of the white sandy beaches. Mix in the swaying palm trees and the amazing sunsets and, for me, this is paradise. Fast-forward many years, and as a mom the greatest gift I can share with my daughter is the gift of travel and my love of the beach. Creating these memories and traditions with her are beyond priceless.

—Ally Genovese

Founder of Ally G's Everyday Angels Foundation

66

Creativity appears in waves;
it transforms us, moves us
from what we once were
into what we can be.
Always stirring, always
changing. Embrace the
changes that come.

KATHERINE IGNATENKO, CREATIVE DIRECTOR, DUNE JEWELRY

99

a lesson in waves

The ocean is a wild and vast ecosystem that sustains itself in the most creative of ways. I'm simply in awe of this glorious creation. Water covers about 70 percent of the Earth's surface and can be up to seven miles deep in some places. Imagine the treasures we would find if we could access the entirety of the ocean? Each layer of water works harmoniously together to sustain various life forms and to provide the air we breathe every day. Songs, books, paintings, architecture, and countless other creative pursuits around the globe are born from humanity's love of the sea.

For me, there is nothing more inspiring than the ocean on a sunny day or a stormy day, at dawn or at dusk. There is always something that will catch your attention and encourage the waves of your imagination to come alive. The vast palette of colors and textures is extraordinary. Think of the sand, whether it's silky soft or crunchy and full of colorful pebbles. The glistening seaweed, gulls overhead, barnacles stuck steadfast to sea rocks, gemlike sea glass and shells sprinkled about, and the infinite salty air creating beach waves in your hair that can never be duplicated. The ocean has the ability to stir the souls of people who have never even set foot on a beach. They've only experienced it through stories and artwork. When we are open and in flow, we allow creativity to move freely like a river running confidently toward the ocean, knowing that its expanse is going to reach far and wide for the world to enjoy.

Creativity is about tapping into our inner selves and recognizing the nature of the people, places, and objects around us. It is the part of our mind that can see magic in the world, and it can create magic too. Have you ever taken a few ingredients in your refrigerator and made a gourmet meal without a recipe? That's your creativity coming out to play. What about when you put an outfit together that's a major head-turner, including hat, shoes, and accessories that all fit seamlessly together—there's that creativity again! Maybe you feel a burst of energy and rearrange your bedroom so that it looks like something out of a magazine. Yep, you guessed it, your creativity has resurfaced. You've probably used creativity throughout your life without even fully realizing it! Whatever your level of creativity, there are always ways to explore what you love and expand your creative horizons.

> BEING CREATIVE ISN'T A "ONE SIZE FITS ALL" CATEGORY. WHETHER YOU RECOGNIZE IT OR NOT, YOU ARE A CREATIVE PERSON.

Just like the ocean wave doesn't ask permission to make its splash, neither should creativity ask permission to make its creation. The beauty of making is in the wild moment, in the motion and emotion of rolling, wrestling, and doing.

HEIDI SCHWARTZ, LIVE EVENT PAINTER

Sometimes, within the chaos of life, we forget to allow ourselves to "play." We neglect to take the time to do things that bring us joy and get us into our flow state. The stress of life, and even our own fears, can stop us from fully embracing our imaginative side. Creativity is not about predictability or perfection—nothing about the ocean is predictable or perfect, yet many of us still find it to be the grandest, most beautiful part of our Earth. Sometimes waves crash into each other as storms form and cause chaos, but the unpredictability makes it even more magnificent.

The ocean creates beauty from the unexpected. Think of sea glass. A bottle is lost at sea, maybe discarded by an irresponsible boater. It's thrown into the ocean and the waves sweep it away, then it's tossed and tumbled for years and years before finally emerging as a softened silhouette, void of the sharp edges it once had. Now considered a thing of beauty, that sea glass looks more like a gemstone than the piece of trash it once was. Creativity comes to us in various ways. You may not find success right away in your creative endeavors, and it may not be perfect, but the end result is a beautiful expression of your artistic journey and that in itself is delightful.

Your "inner child" or playful self can help you tap into your creativity and guide you to a new perspective. Take a few minutes out of your day and do something that requires your imagination. Play with your kids—they have an innate way of bringing us into the present moment. Journal or draw something without overthinking it; work freehand and sketch whatever comes to mind. Take time to go outside, walk your dog, and breathe in the fresh air. Use the moment to notice what you see and what you are grateful for. Do anything that creates that spark in your soul. Start with just two minutes a day and work your way up to five or ten minutes, then as much as you can schedule into your daily life. By creating habits that help you stay in touch with the higher vibrations surrounding you, you will become more open to listening to the inner part of you that is curious and playful.

{ STEP INTO YOURSELF AND SEE WHAT HAPPENS.

The ocean is massive, and so much of it is unexplored. Go to the beach, settle in, and let your imagination run wild. It will unearth the creativity that's already inside of you.

> "

JUST AS THE OCEAN'S WAVES ARE RANDOM AND UNPLANNED, THE FLOW OF CREATIVITY AND IMAGINATION IS FREE, UNCAPPED, AND CAPABLE OF SURPRISING EVEN ITS OWN CREATOR. MY IMAGINATION AND CREATIVITY CAN BE SUDDEN, WAKING ME UP IN THE MIDDLE OF THE NIGHT. BUT THAT'S ALSO THE BEAUTY OF CREATIVITY. YOU NEVER KNOW WHEN IT'LL HIT. JUST LIKE YOU NEVER KNOW WHEN AND WHERE THE OCEAN'S WAVES WILL CRASH.

ADALETA AVDIC, DIGITAL CONTENT CREATOR

"

A WAVE IN
creativity meditation

Find a comfortable position and begin to shift your focus to your breath. Imagine yourself by a peaceful waterside. As you're looking out at the landscape, notice the fine details surrounding you. Let all of your senses start to awaken. What's the time of day? Is it warm or a bit chilly? What color is the sky? Listen closely and hone in on the sounds that are arising from the silence. Feel the Earth supporting your body and notice its texture as you take in the full spectrum of nature before you. Repeat the mantra "I am fully connected with my endless creative source." Take one last deep breath in through your nose and out through your mouth as the picture you've just painted in your mind slowly begins to fade. Start to come back to your body by making gentle circles with your wrists and slowly working movement through the rest of your body. Thank your creative mind for taking you away for a moment and remember that you can always access that energy when you need it the most.

BE
SOULFUL

8

Being by the ocean is the most soulful place I know. The way the ocean rejuvenates the mind, body, and soul is a magical force that can neither be denied nor explained.

sand story

I've had sand between my toes forever. First from the Long Island Sound, then from both Skaket and Nauset Beaches on Cape Cod, then eventually from New Smyrna Beach, Florida. For me, the beach is always the place I go for fun, or for peace, and now to talk to my husband in heaven. Whether it's warm and sunny or cold and gray, the beach clears my head, wipes away my tears, and allows me to put myself back together. The beach transports me to another world. Now my life has come full circle, and I am back where I belong, on Cape Cod! My soul feels grounded again and my toes are delighted to be in these soft, warm sands.

— Patti Kirkman

Wife, Friend, Sand Lover

THE OCEAN IS THE PLACE WHERE
EARTH AND WATER MEET. THE WATER AND
WIND ARE THE ELEMENTS DOING ALL IN THEIR
POWER TO WASH THE BEACH AWAY. BUT
THE BEACH GOES ON AGAINST ALL ODDS.
IT SHOWS US THAT NO MATTER WHAT WE FACE,
BEING MINDFUL AND SOULFUL WILL ALWAYS
ALLOW US TO WEATHER THE ELEMENTS OF LIFE.

MICHELA SOLANCH, CHIEF STRATEGY OFFICER AND PARTNER,
ZERO GRAVITY MARKETING

a lesson in waves

Many people say that the realest version of *you* is found in your soul. It doesn't matter whether you consider yourself religious or spiritual, it's just a feeling you have. You know that there's an essence, a deeper truth behind the person you see in the mirror every day. It's similar to how you can see the ocean as an endless expanse of waves and sea life, but you can *feel* that the ocean is so much more than a simple body of water.

There is something about being in nature that encourages us to get quiet enough to hear the whispers of our soul's longing. It could be in the middle of a vast forest, sitting beside a flowing river, or especially at the ocean's edge, where we are far removed from the worries and cares of our day-to-day duties and responsibilities. Nature is all around us, constantly rebirthing, living, blooming, becoming, and dying. It's the natural rhythm of the universe, and once we tap into it, we will realize that we simply belong here. We don't always have to be working, producing, organizing, caretaking, or creating just to belong. Our soul already belongs. And long after we're gone, our soul's essence lives on. We often feel confined to our own little world, when in reality, we are all connected. We are part of something so much bigger, much grander. Tapping into the vast treasures of the ocean with its many moods, colors, tides, and life-forms helps us unearth our soul's power and purpose. The reflection that the sea provides helps us navigate the depths of our own soul.

In the hustle and bustle of everyday life, it's easy to forget to take the time to get to know who you really are and what your purpose on Earth might be. You know deep down that you aren't the result of aimless, random forces. Something tells you that you were meant for more. You are special and you were born for a reason, even if you have yet to discover your true purpose.

{ KEEPING A PRIVATE JOURNAL IS LIKE A SANCTUARY FOR YOUR SOUL.

One thing that helped me tap into my purpose was consistent journaling. It's a place that no one else will ever see and where no one else can enter unless you invite them. Keep a journal close by, either next to your bed or in your purse or backpack, and write in it as you see fit, preferably at least daily or even a few times a day if the feeling strikes.

Life is forever a journey of learning and growing. In your journey, you may drift away from who you are. But everything is just as it should be, and just like the ocean, the tides of life will always bring your soul back to shore.

KARLI RAE FREDERICKSEN, MODEL, INFLUENCER

It's important to stop what you're doing and express yourself when the feeling comes to you, or the thoughts can disappear as quickly as they arise. By keeping a journal, you can observe yourself evolving over time. You can chart where you've been and where you want to go. A different perspective coming from an external source can cloud your own judgment and stunt you from uncovering your full potential. It can be truly therapeutic to journal out your dreams, wants, needs, visions, thoughts, and inner dialogue without unwarranted input.

{ HAVING A SPACE FREE OF THE THOUGHTS AND OPINIONS OF OTHERS IS A POWERFUL TOOL FOR SELF-REFLECTION.

I still have notebooks from when I began dreaming about my business. There are phrases, logo sketches, rudimentary jewelry designs, nonsensical words that I love strung together with doodled hearts. Most of what is contained in my early journals was more whimsy than work, but it allowed my soul to breathe and opened me up to the possibility of starting my own business. In between drawings of mermaid purses, conch shells, and huge sunflowers are the words "live for the moment, then take it with you." This is a phrase that I still use today. It has stuck with me for over ten years and still to this day helps me define the essence of Dune Jewelry. Going back through these journals and recognizing the manifestation of my business through journaling is honestly a magical experience. The process of building my business was deeply profound for me. Each moment of success and every opportunity to learn connected me more deeply to what feels like my true calling. Being able to flip through my journals and recognize when and where I began to shift my life's path is something I wouldn't trade for the world.

Self-reflection and digging deeper than what feels comfortable will help you uncover your soul's purpose, which is a lifelong journey. What serves you now may not serve you in five or ten years, so it's important to keep an open mind. We humans are constantly absorbing the energy around us—learning, progressing, and acquiring more knowledge to live a fulfilling life.

Be soulful like the ocean: deeply connected, sensitive yet resolute, ever evolving, and perfectly imperfect.

The ocean doesn't hide its emotions. You know when it's calm, you know when it's restless. Like the ocean bares its soul, you can and should too!

BARBARA FARRAGHER, VOICEOVER ARTIST, BROADCASTER BY THE SEA, OCEAN DREAMER

A SOULFUL
wave meditation

Find a comfortable position lying flat on your back. Then close your eyes and focus on your breath. Start to shift your focus inward and begin to imagine a ball of light in the center of your body. Allow the center of your body to begin to feel the warmth of this light and notice as it travels through your body until your entire body is illuminated. Feel this warm bright light extend out into your aura and then even further, as the light of your soul connects with the world around you. This light is ever present in your body and you share it with every other soul you come in contact with. Let this divine connection consume your being until you recognize that you are a part of everything. Hold on to this illuminated feeling as you begin to bring your focus back to your breath. Then slowly begin to come back into your body and open your eyes. Thank your body for being a vessel for your soul and carrying you through this world.

BE
LOVE

BE THE LOVE THAT YOU'VE ALWAYS WANTED TO EXPERIENCE. REMEMBER THE FIRST TIME YOU ENTERED THE OCEAN, REMEMBER FALLING FOR THAT UNDYING EXPERIENCE BETWEEN YOUR HEART AND THE TOUCH AND SOUND OF THE WAVES. BE SO PURE THAT THE UNIVERSE HAS NO OTHER OPTION BUT TO LISTEN TO YOUR WILDEST DESIRES AND GRANT THEM LIBERTY. THAT'S TRUE LOVE.

DY'AMOND BREEDLOVE, NYC STYLIST

sand story

It comes as no surprise that I can tell my story through sand. I grew up a California girl, spending my summers, springs, falls, and winters by the water. I started snorkeling before I was ten, decided to study sea turtles by eleven, got my SCUBA license at thirteen, and moved to the beach at twenty-one. Whenever times got tough, I would head to the beach. The ocean, the sand, the breeze—somehow, they helped me slow down and hear what I needed to move forward. When looking at my life story, four beaches come to mind. The first is Newport Beach, where I fell in love with my husband. Then, a beach in the Bahamas where we got engaged. The third beach in San Francisco is where we started our life together, and the last beach in Galveston is where I spent most of my time while pregnant with our child, Evie. The beach reminds me of who I am, who I've been, and that there's so much more goodness to come.

—Ashley Lopez
Founder and Owner of Simplicity & Coffee

Close your eyes and imagine the salty wind in your hair, the warm sand on your feet, the sun on your face, the scent of the ocean … can you feel it? That is the ocean loving you.

DAISY CABRERA, FINANCIAL WIZARD, JEWELRY LOVER

a lesson in waves

Picture self-love like the ocean to the moon. During a calm, peaceful sea, the moon looks down at the ocean and sees its reflection as gloriously bright, lighting up the world for all to admire. Other times, the sea is tempestuous and dark, and the moon sees a distorted vision of itself, cloudy, rippled, and flawed. This does not mean that the moon is ultimately flawed; it means that circumstances have temporarily tampered with the moon's perception of itself. The ocean will change time and time again, as will our life's circumstances, and while our appearance and credo may change as the moon's outward look does, it does not mean that we have changed at our core. We are beautiful and worthy creatures that deserve to love and be loved.

Accessing your own self-love is not always constant; it is an appreciation for yourself that develops over time from practices that support your growth—physical, mental, and spiritual. Self-love means having a healthy attitude toward your own well-being and trusting your intuition. Loving yourself requires putting your own needs first and not sacrificing them to gain the approval of others. It means having a healthy ego, knowing your worth, and not settling for leftovers. Loving yourself does not mean that you're selfish or narcissistic, no matter what others might believe.

Of course, self-love means different things to different people, and we all have unique avenues and practices to establish a solid foundation. It doesn't come naturally to many people, especially those who have been marginalized due to their race, gender, sexual orientation, and other external factors. Our culture has been shaped by aggressive white males, and for years it has rewarded Type A personality characteristics even when it didn't make sense. Thankfully, the world is beginning to transform. Learning who we are at our core and fully embracing what we deserve will continue to enact positive change.

> DETERMINING WHAT SELF-LOVE MEANS TO YOU IS AN IMPORTANT PART OF THE JOURNEY.

It can be tough to shift your inner dialogue from a place of criticism to a place of love and appreciation. If you're having trouble cultivating more self-love in your life, take the time to practice some of the following habits.

Practice more positive self-talk, both internal and out loud. Finding fault with your past actions instead of striving to do better in the future is a sure sign that you're being too critical of yourself.

Plunging into the cool, salty ocean, our souls are replenished and renewed with confidence, love, happiness, and peace. Nature's patience surrounds us.

KRISTINE CRUGNALE, EDUCATOR

If you find that you are criticizing yourself or talking negatively about yourself too often, practice saying something encouraging. It can be about your physical body, your personality, or a skill you possess. One thing that I do just about every night before bed is to repeat the mantra "I love myself unconditionally and without judgment" over and over until I fall asleep. This small habit helps me tremendously when I feel like I've made a bad decision or I sense regret creeping in. Also, look in the mirror each morning and say at least one good thing to your reflection with a big, genuine smile. If you can make this a habit, I promise that you'll notice a shift in how you see yourself.

> BE NICE TO YOURSELF, AND HONOR YOUR THOUGHTS AND IDEAS BY TRUSTING YOUR OWN WISDOM.

The more you empower yourself to make decisions and follow your intuition, the more accountable you become for your own life. Trust your internal "gut" feelings. Stop the second-guessing and judgment that leads to guilt, shame, and regret. I personally don't identify with the word *regret*. I struck it from my inner dialogue years ago when I was healing from the embarrassment of my upbringing. Even now when I make a decision that is deemed a "failure," I don't regret it. Living in the past is what brings me anxiety and grief, and it doesn't serve my evolution. I learn, I fail forward, and I move on.

Prioritize and balance your wants and needs against those of others. Healthy boundaries will determine what you are and are not willing to do. Part of setting boundaries is learning to say no, which is a key component of leading a balanced life. You can't be all things to all people if you want to preserve your sense of self-worth. The other part to setting healthy boundaries requires evaluating your relationships. Assess the toxic behaviors of the people in your life and create healthy boundaries for yourself and your relationship with your loved ones to keep yourself feeling safe and loved. In other words, *protect your energy*.

Self-love is a factor in motivating you to make healthy life choices. When you have high self-esteem, you are more likely to choose actions that enhance your confidence rather than diminish it. It can be as simple as an outfit that makes you feel empowered, or carving out time in the morning for an elaborate skin care routine that tells your inner self, "This is my day, my life, and I'm the most important person to take care of today." When you improve your relationship with yourself, quite often the relationships with those around you begin to flourish as well.

It's time to acknowledge that *you* are the main character of your life's story.

Let's ride this wave of love, I'll take you to the ocean, it's just a feeling from above, it's higher, it's higher.

"WAVE OF LOVE," POP ROCK BAND HELLO SISTER

A WAVE IN
love meditation

Use this heart-opening meditation to allow yourself to be open to love in all its forms. Lie down on a comfortable surface and place a bolster or rolled-up towel vertically behind your back so that your shoulders fall to the sides, opening your heart space. If this is too uncomfortable, feel free to lie flat on your back. Place one hand on your belly and the other on your chest. Close your eyes and begin to breathe in and out, taking long, deep breaths. Send the air into your belly and feel your hand as it begins to rise, continuing to fill your lungs as the hand over your chest begins to rise as well. Exhale. Say, "I love myself unconditionally and without judgment." Repeat this mantra for as long as you like. Once you are finished, slowly open your eyes and begin to move your fingers, toes, wrists, and ankles. When you are ready, roll over onto your side and push yourself up into a sitting position. Give love to your mind and body for all they do for you.

BE
GROUNDED

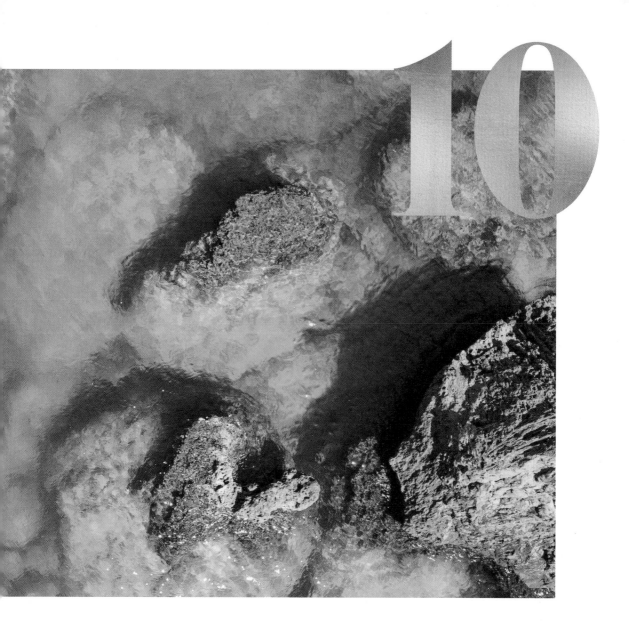

Even when the surface of the sea is full of monstrous waves, the depths of the sea remain undisturbed. This is a reminder that in the midst of life's storms, there can still be peace in the depths of one's soul.

JASMIN GRAHAM, MARINE BIOLOGIST

sand story

My house and my mother were taken from me at a young age, so I never truly felt tied to one place. My mom was the one who taught me how to love the beach. Warm summer days at White Horse Beach in Plymouth, Massachusetts, are remembered with her laughter—I can close my eyes and see her sitting on a big rock at low tide looking into the sunset. I've always felt more connected to her sitting in the sand watching the seagulls chase a crab than anywhere else. Throughout my life, becoming a friend of mine meant spending a day at White Horse. From sunbathing with my high school girlfriends to wilder times on the beach in my twenties, it's been a staple of my life. I always lament when it's time to shake out the beach blanket and pack up. My heart is always fuller when I'm at White Horse—it's my home.

—*Lauren Behning*
Brand Manager, Dune Jewelry

THE OCEAN HAS ALWAYS BEEN A METAPHORICAL
PLACE FOR ME TO GROUND MYSELF. AS I STARE
AT THE WAVES AND MEDITATE, I AM REMINDED
THAT EACH WAVE CRASHING ONTO THE SAND IS
REMINISCENT OF MY PROBLEMS. THEY DISSIPATE.
THEY SEEM SO GRAND AND THEN FADE. PRESSURE
FROM THE WEIGHT OF THE MASS BEHIND IT
SURFACES AND BECOMES EFFORTLESSLY NOTHING.
NONEXISTENT. THIS GROUNDS ME TO REMEMBER
THAT EVERYTHING I PERCEIVE AS SERIOUS OR
WEIGHTED WILL ONE DAY HOLD NO FORM.

RACHAEL SHTIFTER, CEO OF PARLR,
PARLR BRAND STUDIO & SLEEPY TIE

a lesson in waves

Whenever I am visiting a warm location, without fail the first thing I do in the morning is walk out the front door and let my bare feet find the earth. Think of how it feels to walk calmly on a warm stone walkway, then sink your toes into the soft sand of a beach that you love. Feel a sense of peaceful focus—take a breath, find your footing, and enjoy the feeling of being present, grounded, and well balanced. Don't think about your external problems; just let your feet enjoy the sensation of the sand and the sound of the waves crashing to shore. When you allow this tranquility to wash over you and ground yourself in the present moment, you are able to center your thoughts and feel an overwhelming sense of clarity. When you are grounded, you are focused, clear, and calm, and you make better decisions that don't stem solely from emotion.

At its simplest level, being grounded means that you can weather any storm that comes your way. You're comfortable with who you are, confident and calm. When everyone else is trying to live up to the expectations of others, you are anchored to your inner dialogue and life choices. Despite living in a world full of uncertainty, you know that you've made choices that will serve you best and you are able to enjoy the present moment without focusing too much on the past or future.

Someone who is not grounded is apt to sway whichever way the wind is blowing. They are prone to latch on to outside influences, or worse yet, to let the opinions of others dictate their reality in unhealthy ways. Lack of grounding can also show up in the way you carry yourself day to day. Being easily triggered or thrown off balance by an off-the-cuff remark or incident like being cut off on the highway can be far more dramatic than it needs to be. There's an impatience and lack of emotional control.

> WE NEED TO FOCUS OUR ATTENTION ON WHAT IS HAPPENING IN THE HERE AND NOW RATHER THAN ON THE "WHAT MIGHT HAVE BEEN."

Studies show that about 85 percent of our worries will never come to pass. The past and future do not actually exist. All we have is the present moment. Wasting the present moment on something that may never happen keeps us from the joy and thrill of what is happening right in front of us.

As long as her feet are grounded in the sand, a woman can conquer any wave that comes her way, no matter how fierce or unpredictable it may be.

CHRISTINA THOMPSON, FOUNDER/CEO, GOLF4HER.COM, 2X CANCER SURVIVOR

There are many physical ways to ground your body and your mental state. One is through a process called "grounding" or "earthing." This is a healing technique that has to do with physically reconnecting yourself to the Earth. It's a simple practice of connecting to nature by being outside and immersing yourself in the beauty of the outdoors—in its simplest form, it is the feeling of your feet on the ground connecting with the Earth. You can have a grounding experience by participating in outdoor activities such as visiting a garden and picking vegetables, or listening to the wind blowing through the leaves. If you don't have a backyard or green space to practice in, you can drive to a park or lake and walk barefoot. If that's not feasible, carry grounding oils that you can smell, such as frankincense, vetiver, or sandalwood. The process of taking the time to stop and smell these grounding oils is enough to center your thoughts for the day.

Earthing science and grounding physics are finding that conditions such as inflammation, cardiovascular disease, muscle damage, chronic pain, and negative moods can all be improved through grounding. And the research is just getting started. Nature is literally healing you when you don't even realize it. Negative ions are odorless, tasteless molecules that we inhale in abundance in certain environments. Mountain trails, waterfalls, beaches, lakes, and ponds all have plentiful negative ions. Once they reach our bloodstream, they produce biochemical reactions that increase levels of serotonin in the brain, which helps alleviate stress and depression and boosts energy. Negative ions are also said to counter the effects of free radicals that can break down our immune system. Pretty incredible, right?

> RECOGNIZING THAT YOU CAN BE SERENE AND AT PEACE EVEN IN THE MIDST OF TURMOIL WILL SERVE YOU WELL.

The ability to stay calm, present, and focused even during negative situations is a really powerful tool, whether you're a student, mom, or business owner. It will serve you through difficult moments in your life. It's not easy, but it's important to find time to ground yourself so that you can bring more abundance into your life. When chaos takes over, it's hard to see the light at the end of the tunnel, but when you tune in to your natural rhythm, you have the ability to enjoy the present moment. Being present has been shown to perpetuate happiness and improve memory. When you're doing or thinking too many things at once, memories seem to fade away quickly, but when you're grounded, memories stick with you longer, which is a true gift.

In times of uncertainty, be strong like the tide, let the waves move you, and breathe in the ocean air. You will find clarity in the beauty of the sea.

NICOLE QUINN, FASHION BLOGGER, BEHAVIOR ANALYST

A GROUNDING
wave meditation

For this meditation you'll need to get outside and find a patch of grass, soil, or sand to connect with. Stand up straight or sit in a chair with your feet touching the ground. Close your eyes as you begin to deepen your breath. Focus on the sensation of the ground under your feet. Feel the energetic connection between the Earth and your body. You are fully safe and supported by the ground beneath you. Allow the grounding energy to travel through your feet and move up your legs, arms, torso, and all the way to the top of your head. Repeat the mantra "I am safe and supported; I am grounded" as you take a few more deep breaths in and out. Imagine your body is so deeply connected to the Earth that it has planted roots beneath you. Slowly begin to open your eyes and take in your surroundings. Thank the Earth for its calming and supportive energy. This practice sets you up for a grounded and focused day.

> NOW MORE THAN EVER IT'S IMPORTANT
> FOR US TO BE A VOICE FOR THE VOICELESS
> CREATURES UNDER THE SURFACE OF THE SEA.
> EVERYTHING WE DO HAS AN IMPACT ON OUR
> ENVIRONMENT. EVERY DISPOSABLE ITEM THAT
> ISN'T PROPERLY RECYCLED COULD EASILY
> END UP IN OUR OCEANS. WE HAVE THE POWER
> TO STOP IT AND IT STARTS WITH REDUCING
> CONSUMPTION AND GETTING RID OF
> SINGLE-USE PLASTICS. LET'S COLLECTIVELY
> BE THAT VOICE TO ENACT CHANGE.

CAMILLE KOSTEK, ACTRESS, TELEVISION HOST,
OCEAN ADVOCATE

SAVE A WAVE

The ocean covers more than 70 percent of the Earth's surface and is essential to the health of our planet. Climate change, pollution, and a simple lack of awareness continue to put oceanic resources at risk. Every move you make, whether large or small, can help. There is still time to heal our planet but we must take purposeful action immediately. The time is now.

In this section you will find tips, tricks, and resources separated into different categories to help you discover things that you can do to help our environment.

Groceries and Purchasing Items

- **BUY IN BULK!** Dry goods, cleaning supplies, and beauty products like shampoo and conditioner can all be bought in bulk. This helps reduce wasteful packaging and multiple trips to the grocery store.

- **WASH OUT AND REUSE JARS AND GLASS CONTAINERS.** Salsa jars, coconut oil jars, peanut butter jars—save them all. Most of these jars are super sturdy, spill-proof, and airtight.

- **PRACTICE MEATLESS MONDAY.** This encourages people to reduce meat in their diet for the health of the planet. It's also great for your personal health.

- **SKIP THE DRINKS IN PLASTIC BOTTLES.** Choose a glass option or try your best to carry a reusable water bottle at all times.

- **REDUCE BUYING COFFEE TO GO.** That drink lid could live on for over a hundred years. Brew your coffee at home and take it with you in a reusable cup.

- **CHALLENGE YOURSELF TO CUT DOWN ON EATING OUT.** Create delicious meals at home and eat those leftovers. The average American household contributes 500 pounds of food waste per year.

- **GROW YOUR OWN FOOD OR VISIT YOUR LOCAL FARMERS' MARKET.** Buying local means your food doesn't have to travel thousands of miles to get to you, which saves on fossil fuels and carbon emissions.

Household Items

- **TAKE A LOOK** at the products you use at home every day and slowly swap out wasteful items with Earth-friendly options.

- **CREATE AN "OOPS" JAR** for the moments you leave the house without your reusable items. If you grab a coffee but you forgot your reusable cup or straw, put a dollar in your oops jar.

- **IF YOU HAVE A DISHWASHER, USE IT.** Washing dishes by hand can use up to 27 gallons of water while your dishwasher will only use 3 to 5 gallons of water. Plus, it's a little less work on your end.

- **SWAP FROM DRYER SHEETS TO WOOL DRYER BALLS.** Dryer sheets are a single-use product filled with harmful chemicals. Wool dryer balls are chemical free and can last up to a thousand wash cycles.

- **CONSIDER USING SAFETY RAZORS INSTEAD OF PLASTIC ONES.** Plastic razors and razor heads are nearly impossible to recycle.

- **CONSIDER SWITCHING TO A MENSTRUAL CUP INSTEAD OF USING TAMPONS OR PADS.** A menstrual cup can last for years, and you never run out when you need it!

- **SWAP MAKEUP WIPES** and cotton rounds with facecloths.

- **SWITCH ALL OF YOUR LIGHT BULBS TO LED BULBS.** LED bulbs are up to 80 percent more energy efficient than your standard light bulb.

- **GO PAPERLESS!** Most companies now have online billing options.

Clothing

- **WEAR YOUR CLOSET!** Challenge yourself for three months to refrain from purchasing any new clothing or accessories. This will help you weed out of your closet all the things you'll never wear, and simultaneously hone your style. You can donate items that you don't wear or give them to a friend.

- **GO THRIFTING!**

- **SET UP A CLOTHING SWAP WITH FRIENDS.** We all love to wear new things, and wouldn't it be great if we could do so without spending any money or hurting the environment? Find a friend with similar style and sizing and coordinate a clothing swap every other month.

Other Things You Can Do

- **COMPOSTING** is a great way to recycle kitchen waste.

- **COMMUTE, CARPOOL, OR BIKE** to work if those options are accessible to you.

- **ONCE A MONTH GO FOR A TRASH WALK.** Hit your favorite beach, a hiking trail you love, or just walk around your neighborhood with a trash bag and fill it up, then dispose of it properly.

- **SUPPORT GREAT ORGANIZATIONS** that are fighting for the future of our oceans. If you could donate time, money, or resources to any of the following, it would be a great start:

  - Bye Bye Plastic Bags
  - Coral Reef Alliance
  - Greenpeace
  - Lonely Whale

  - Marine Fish Conservation Network
  - Mission Blue
  - Oceana
  - Surfrider Foundation

- **CHALLENGE YOURSELF TO CARVE OUT TECH-FREE TIME** for at least one hour a day. Read, write, draw, color, or get outside. You'll save at least an hour's worth of electric energy by staying off of screens and you'll find it will boost your mood as well.

- **THE MORE KNOWLEDGE WE HAVE ABOUT MOTHER EARTH,** the more likely we are to fall in love and keep her safe. Here's a short list of documentaries and series that will help expand your knowledge and keep you entertained at the same time:

  - *A Plastic Ocean*
  - *Chasing Coral*
  - David Attenborough's *Blue Planet I* and *II*

  - *Down to Earth*
  - *Mission Blue*
  - *My Octopus Teacher*

SAND BANK

Here's a short list of sands from around the world. To check out more sands, visit Dune Jewelry's website at https://dunejewelry.com/.

Bali
Indonesia

Iwo Jima
Japan

Jökulsárlón
Iceland

Warwick Long Bay Beach
Bermuda

Jetties Beach
Nantucket, Massachusetts

Amadores Beach
Canary Islands

Harbour Island
Bahamas

Myrtos Beach
Kefalonia, Greece

Cinque Terre
Liguria, Italy

Glass Beach
Fort Bragg, California

George Dog Island
British Virgin Islands

South Sounds
Grand Cayman

Magens Bay
St. Thomas, Caribbean

Mustang Island
Texas

Frisco Beach
Outer Banks, North Carolina

Beach Haven
Jersey Shore, New Jersey

Sanibel Island
Florida

Edisto Island
South Carolina

Fajã Grande
Azores, Portugal

Erg Chebbi Sand Dunes
Morocco

Cape Verde
West Africa

Surfers Paradise Beach
Gold Coast, Australia

Motutapu Island
New Zealand

Perkins Cove
Ogunquit, Maine

Prince Edward Island
Canada

Malpais
Puntarenas, Costa Rica

Cape Evans
Ross Island, Antarctica

Eagle Beach
Juneau, Alaska

Boca Grandi
San Nicolas, Aruba

Cabo San Lucas
Mexico

Dorado Beach
Puerto Rico

Bavaro Beach
Punta Cana, Dominican Republic

Longberry Beach
Dominica

South Friars Bay
St. Kitts and Nevis

St. Jean Beach
St. Barts

Plage de l'Almanarre
France

Long Beach
Washington State

Kappil Beach
Bekal, India

Vohemar
Madagascar

women featured

Becca Lee @beccaleepoetry

Samantha Robshaw @srobshawphoto

Nicole Michelle @nicolemichellesings

Amber Jewel Wax @amberjewelstyle

Nicole Borriello @nicole_theresas_lair

Nicole Amato @amatostyle

Katie Simpson @ksyogasuffolk

Joli Boucher

Caroline Karwoski @carolinekarwoski

Kate Colozzi @katecolozzi

Teri Tkachuk @stellargirlofficial

Vanessa Coppes @vanessacoppes

Raina Patricia

Georgia Shurtleff @georgiashurtleff

Linda Burke

Marilyn Ball @speakingoftravel

Lauren Behning @sharkbitestudio

Deanne Capotosto @deannecap

Danielle Godjikian @mellowdanyellow_

Moira Garcia @moira2garcia

Tiffany Rice @spirittiff

Jennifer DeCillis @jennifer.decillis

Suzanne Dwyer @tpbdcoach

Courtenay Cooper Hall @courtenayhall

Carole Imperiale @caroleimp

Dawn Del Russo @dawndelrusso

Jen Mueller

Cheldin Barlatt Rumer @cheldinbarlatt

Candace Cross @candiceaurus

Katherine Ignatenko @kth_ign

Heidi Schwartz @paintyourevent

Adaleta Avdic @adaatude

Ally Genovese @allygseverydayangelsfoundation

Julie Fairweather @dirtywatermedia

Michela Solanch @michelasolanch

Karli Rae Fredericksen @karliraefredericksen

Barbara Farragher @smilingvoice

Patti Kirkman

Dy'amond Breedlove @dyamondbreedlovenyc

Daisy Cabrera @daisycabrera64

Kristine Crugnale

Hello Sister @hellosistermusic

Ashley Lopez @simplicityandcoffee

Jasmin Graham Twitter: @Elasmo_Gal

Rachael Shtifter @rachlynsey

Christina Thompson @golf4her

Nicole Quinn @nikkisfashion411

Camille Kostek @camillekostek

references

"10 Unbelievable Facts About the Ocean." The Real Word from Trafalgar, August 2020. https://www.trafalgar.com/real-word/10-unbelievable-facts-ocean.

Mann, Denise. "Negative Ions Create Positive Vibes." WebMD, May 2002. https://www.webmd.com/balance/features/negative-ions-create-positive-vibes.

Menigoz, Wendy, Tracy Latz, Robin Ely, Cimone Kamei, Gregory Melving, and Drew Sinatra. "Integrative and Lifestyle Medicine Strategies Should Include Earthing (Grounding): Review Research Evidence and Clinical Observations." Explore 16, no. 3 (May–June 2020): 152–160. https://pubmed.ncbi.nlm.nih.gov/31831261.

acknowledgments

Thank you to everyone who has supported me unconditionally since day one of my entrepreneurial journey. I'm infinitely grateful.

To my Dune Dream Team, I'm so lucky to work with each and every one of you. You make going to work every day something that I love.

To all of my Wave Makers out there— you are the best! Keep experiencing life like every day is your last. I'll be here to celebrate with you and capture your memories in a tangible reminder that you can carry with you forever.

Dustin Bell, thank you for helping me build Dune Jewelry since day one. We've had twelve years of learning, growth, strength, and perseverance.

Maggie Scanlon, you're a game-changer! Let's keep growing and learning together.

Kate Colozzi, from dancing on the bar at Coyote Ugly to chic dinners with clients after trade shows—twenty-plus years of friendship and now being colleagues just works for us. I won the life lottery when I met you, and I'm thankful every day.

Lauren Behning, my confidante. We're eight years in, with a lifetime to go. Wait until you see what we build together. Your star is so bright and it's only just starting to shine. Your potential is limitless.

Carole Imperiale, who would have thought that a simple PR pitch email would lead us on a journey to become lifelong friends? You're my rock—always so strong, and pushing me out of my comfort zone because you always see my potential. Your "never say never" attitude and pleasantly persistent nature is a dream.

Katherine Ignatenko, your endless creativity, strong vision, and commitment to making Dune a powerhouse brand astounds me every day. Words can't express how grateful I am to have you on my team.

Samantha Robshaw, thirty-plus years and counting. Can you imagine what our twelve-year-old selves would say to us right now? I think they'd be very, very proud. Thank you for sticking with me and always being my biggest cheerleader.

Daisy Cabrera, you're a gift sent from heaven. I've said that since day one. Thank you for all you do every single day.

Moira Garcia, your tenacity and talent leaves me in awe. Thank you for always working so hard and building this business with such passion. You are a gift!

Kellie Quinn, my sister—a lifetime together and here we are. Your creative vision is extraordinary, and I'm so happy that it's brought us full circle. The future is bright!

Jeff Taraschi, thank you for always doing your best to keep our ship sailing in the right direction. Shoulder to shoulder

Ally G., you are the most inspirational, energetic angel. Thank you for being part of my team.

Thank you to my collaborators, Camille Kostek, Nicole Michelle, Ann Liguori, Tiffany Rice, and Dy'amond Breedlove.

Thank you to Andrea Dulski for helping to keep my home life in order. Laundry could easily be the demise of a Mom CEO!

Thank you to Rage Kindelsperger, Keyla Pizzaro-Hernández, and the Quarto team for making this dream a reality.

And to all of the inspiring women in my family who have supported every moment—Debbie Christensen, Cathy McManus, Linda Santamaria, Jeannie Caputo, Lisa Sinibaldi, Pam, Lauren, Lizzy and Stephanie LeBlanc, Kristie, Courtney and Stephanie McManus, Deb Banks, Janet Daniels, and Toni Clark.

about the author

HOLLY DANIELS CHRISTENSEN is a mom, travel lover, and kitchen table entrepreneur who has propelled her business, Dune Jewelry & Co., from a passion project to a worldwide brand over the past eleven years. Holly is unafraid of hard work and possesses an inspirational "never say never" attitude. She is a talented designer focused on capturing memories to create tangible reminders of life's most cherished moments, which symbolizes Dune's line of handcrafted Experiential Jewelry.® As the recipient of many awards, she is a self-proclaimed "work in progress" and credits the healing power of the ocean for much of her evolution from high school dropout to well-respected and successful CEO. An advocate for giving back to the community, Holly is proud to spearhead many fundraisers each year for nonprofit organizations. She lives outside of Boston, Massachusetts, with her husband Eric, two young daughters Lexa and Lyla, and their trusty rescue pup, Earle. To connect with Holly, check out her website at https://dunejewelry.com/ or her Instagram @holly_daniels_christensen and @dunejewelry.